Encourage-Mints

Encourage-Mints

GIVE A MINT ~ REFRESH A LIFE

Carol Freed

Web sites by Carol Freed: www.newchristian.info www.basicfamily.org
ISBN: 1516964616
ISBN 13: 9781516964611

Dedication

§

Dedicated to anyone, anywhere, who acts on their belief

that one person can make a difference,

connecting with others to influence the present

and impact the future. Keep on being the one!

It is from the numberless diverse acts of courage

and belief that human history is shaped.

Each time a man stands up for an ideal,

or acts to improve the lot of others,

or strikes out against injustice,

he sends forth a tiny ripple of hope,

and crossing each

other from a million

different centers of energy and daring,

those ripples build a current that can

sweep down the mightiest walls

of oppression and resistance.

Spoken to the people of South Africa by

Robert Kennedy in June 1966.

These words are engraved in stone

by his grave in Arlington National Cemetery.

Table of Contents

Free Online Encourage-Mints For You

Let everything you say be good and helpful

so that your words will be an encouragement

to those who hear them.

Ephesians 4:29 NLT

What Is An Encourage-Mint?

§

My dear brothers and sisters, be strong and immovable.

Always work enthusiastically for the Lord, for you know that

nothing you do for the Lord is ever useless.

I Corinthians 15:58 NLT

Kind words can be short and easy to speak,

but their echoes are truly endless.

Mother Teresa

We can't help everyone,

but everyone can help someone.

President Ronald Reagan

EVERYDAY LIFE INVOLVES MANY WAYS to become discouraged, worried and afraid. Sarcasm, cruel words and heartless actions infect everyone. We can't escape the negative influences all around us.

People are searching for encouragement ~ there is a huge need. Google the word "encourage" and you get millions of results.

So with all that endless information available, why write this book? To share a simple way to bring kindness and hope to people you meet with guidance from the Holy Spirit. Hebrews 10:24 reminds us to think of ways to motivate one another to acts of love and good works.

Many articles, books and movies have talked about paying it forward, random acts of kindness and making a difference. However, when these are done without God, a person could be trying to boost their self-esteem to impress others. A person might even be trying to show God how "good" they are - so God will love them more. Thankfully, God's love is a gift we do not need to earn.

Encourage-mints are unique because they include asking God to show you who to talk to and then trusting He will give you the perfect words or help that specific person needs at that exact time. Encourage-mints are not random or coincidence or accidental. They are part of God's plan for our lives.

Candy mints comes in all sizes and shapes. Tiny mints quickly melt in your mouth compared to a larger after-meal mint that takes several minutes to dissolve slowly. Mint inside chocolate, inside a shiny green wrapper, left on a bed pillow gives a quick burst of flavors that says, "Welcome. Enjoy your stay with us." Some mints have wrappers with messages meant to be as uplifting as the mint is refreshing.

Just like those candy mints, encourage-mints come in endless forms and provide a mixture of effects and influence on those who receive them. Through these mints, you become a touch from God that he uses to show his love to people beat up by the world. Unfortunately in our culture, all forms of media often portray Christians as judgmental and hypocrites ~ just plain scary. Therefore, we need to be real-life examples of Jesus' love, kindness, mercy and peace through our words and actions.

This book gives you stories of how I have seen encourage-mints work in my life and provides ideas of what it could be like in your daily life when you follow the promptings of the Holy Spirit to reach out to others.

The more you encourage, the more it will become a natural part of who you are and how you live ~ an enjoyable habit.

We can best prepare ourselves to be an encourager because we have first been encouraged through God's word. As a Christian, I believe in the God of the Holy Bible, a trinity of three persons in one God with specific purposes:

Father ~ creator of the universe ~ everything ~
including people ~ and He keeps it all going

Son ~ Jesus Christ ~ died for my sins so I am forgiven
and will have eternal life with God ~
as a man, He showed us what God is really like

Holy Spirit ~ lives inside us, also called the helper,
his quiet inner voice gives us hope,
guidance and understanding of Jesus and the Bible

We can learn a lot about how the Holy Spirit is part of our lives in the Epistles, the books of the New Testament in the Bible. These letters were written by people who lived with Jesus and witnessed his life, death and resurrection, and by Paul, the apostle (teacher) whom Jesus called to be his spokesman.

Remember that learning about God is a lifetime exploration, so don't wait until you think you know enough or have enough training to be an encourager. Part of the adventure of being a Christian is that God can and does use anyone who is willing.

Acquire knowledge so you can take action. Read books that give fuel to your faith. Listen to speakers who point you to Jesus, whose love is unconditional and provides the best motivation for how to live your life. Hang around people who celebrate you, not just tolerate you. See them as a blessing from God.

We've all heard the phrase, "What's in it for me?" When you follow the light of Jesus Christ, you change that to say, "It's not all about me."

After you have seen the light, you can no longer tolerate the darkness.

The Starfish Story

A young girl was walking along a beach upon which thousands of starfish had been washed up during a terrible storm. When she came to each starfish, she would pick it up and throw it back into the ocean. People watched her with amusement.

She had been doing this for some time when a man approached her and said, "Little girl, why are you doing this? Look at this beach! You can't save all these starfish. You can't begin to make a difference!"

The girl seemed crushed, suddenly deflated. But after a few moments, she bent down, picked up another starfish, and hurled it as far as she could into the ocean. Then she looked up at the man and replied, "Well, I made a difference to that one!"

The old man looked at the girl inquisitively and thought about what she had done and said. Inspired, he joined the little girl in throwing starfish back into the sea. Soon others joined, and all the starfish were saved.

From www.wikipedia.org the online encyclopedia

"The Star Thrower" (or "starfish story") is part of a 16-page essay of the same name by Loren Eiseley (1907–1977), published in 1969 in The Unexpected Universe. It is also the title of a 1978 anthology of Eiseley's works (including the essay), which he completed shortly before his death. The story has been adapted and retold by motivational speakers and on internet sites, often without attribution, since at least the mid-1980s.

Prayer Bears On Duty

To be a Christian without prayer is no more possible

than to be alive without breathing.

Martin Luther

The prayer of a righteous person is powerful and effective.

James 5:16 – NIV

If we don't know what to pray, it doesn't matter.

God's spirit does our praying in and for us, making

prayer out of our wordless sighs and aching groans.

He knows us far better than we know ourselves.

Romans 8:26 The Message

My close friend was starting chemotherapy for a cancer that would all too soon win the battle for her life. I wished it were possible for me to sit beside her and hold her hand as the IV line pumped chemicals into her weak body.

What could I do to encourage her at this painful time in her life? That's when the idea came to me for my first "prayer bear." Why not give her a Teddy bear to keep her company? Unconditional love given through the power of touching a soft, cuddly, stuffed animal. So comforting that paramedics and ER staff often give a huggable bear to a child who has gone through a traumatic event.

I carefully shopped and found a cute, small, white bear. Its paws and feet had bright red fabric with white hearts on it, and the same fabric was tied into a bow around its neck. My friend unwrapped the bear and smiled as she hugged it.

I explained to her that it was a prayer bear on duty, to be with her at the chemo treatments. Whenever she looked at it or held it, she was to remember the people who loved her and were praying for her. The next time I saw her, she said the bear gave her comfort and did remind her of the love of her friends and family.

Since then, I have lovingly chosen more prayer bears and given them to other people going through tough times. Even men have appreciated them. Our neighbor's wife said that her husband insisted his bear sit on the table by his bed, whether at home or at the hospital.

My friend Nita received one of my prayer bears. She is a normally non-stop amazing woman who was suddenly bedridden, weak and barely able to walk, fighting to recover from a fall.

"When Carol came into my bedroom and gave me a prayer bear, I held it close to me and put it in bed next to me. I carried it from room to room and slept with it at night.

The reminder played in my mind and heart each time I saw it or felt it in my bed – *people are praying for me.*"

My friend Jeanie received a bear while her husband was undergoing open heart surgery.

"At the time, the bear became my comforter. I took it everywhere with me, even to bed.

I kept telling myself that it was nothing but a stuffed toy, but I could not ignore it. I would talk to it, sing to it and cuddle it. My husband had complications, and this little stuffed toy heard all my fears and lay beside me when I cried. After we knew that my husband was OK and I could bring him home from the hospital, I put the bear next to my computer. Now several years later, the bear still holds a special place in my heart and sits where I can see him every day."

Yet prayer bears are not only for someone who is sick or suffering from a life crisis. Our grandchildren each were given a prayer bear – to remind them that their Granny prays for them often.

By giving comfort through these cuddly bears, you provide a hug from God. So who do you know that needs your encouragemint of a prayer bear on duty?

Close Encounters Of The God Kind

People may forget what you said or did,

but people will never forget how you made them feel.

Mayou Angelou

Lord, what do you want me to do? asked Saul.

Acts 9:6 NKJ

If you think you are too small to make a difference,

you haven't spent the night with a mosquito.

African proverb

WE DON'T NEED TO LIVE in the *Twilight Zone* to experience the mystery and thrill of giving an encourage-mint to a person we unexpectedly meet, at a time and place we had not planned.

Many years ago, I realized friends and strangers talked with me beyond a simple, "Hi, how are you?" They would quickly tell me about something serious happening in their lives. Perhaps they sensed I was a safe person who could be trusted not to pass along their story to anyone else. Perhaps they sensed I would give them a verbal, and sometimes physical, hug. Perhaps they needed to shed a few tears and not have to appear "brave" around me.

Whatever our physical environment, we would suddenly find ourselves transported to a place of deeper conversation that could only have been orchestrated by God. These random encounters were more than a quirk of fate, coincidence or chance get-togethers.

As a result of these experiences, I often ask my heavenly father to open my eyes and heart to the person he wants me to touch with his love that day. This attitude of expectation makes it easier to recognize the person God intended for me to give an encourage-mint.

Years ago at a large youth event, I was exhausted from the August heat. I thought about walking to my car in the parking lot during the lunch break, turning on the air-conditioner and taking a short nap. But the Holy Spirit had other plans. A young woman came over to me and said that she recognized me as a PTA volunteer at our sons' middle school. Since over 25,000 people were at the event held in another state, having anyone recognize me there was surprising!

She said, "I have watched how you handle your sons and see the respect you have for each other. Our family life resembles a battlefield with our teen. Could I talk to you about this?" Her story involved a problem I had experienced, so I was able to gently suggest a few ideas that might help their family dynamics. She thanked me, gave me a big hug, and hurried off into the crowd.

If I had refused to talk with her, thought only of my comfort level and ignored the quiet urging of the Holy Spirit, this important conversation would not have happened. The benefit to me? I was no longer tired and easily had enough energy and enthusiasm to finish the day's events without a nap. The benefit to her and her family? I gladly leave those results to God.

After living in the same small town for 40 years, I often meet someone familiar, which makes it easier to talk with them. But what if a person lives in or visits a town where everyone is a stranger? Why bother talking to someone you probably will never see again? Understandably, we could choose to remain anonymous. Yet, if we have covered our day with prayer, our mental attitude and sense of caring take on God's perspective. We are available and can enjoy our chances to be used by God to help others.

Maybe you have a seemingly endless "to-do" list of errands and quickly rush from one place to another. Yet everything takes longer than planned and slows you down, leading to more and more frustration. Then you hear the Holy Spirit in your thoughts saying every distraction has been leading you to meet with a special person right then. So you look around ~ and you just know who it is!

You could be with another parent at a school event, or reading a magazine in a doctor's waiting room, and that special person sits down beside you with a deep sigh or teary eyes. Thank God for this close encounter, and trust the Holy Spirit to give you the right words to say or action to take. Without a doubt, when I have been willing to give an encourage-mint, God always provided enough time and energy to almost miraculously get my other "important" things done that day.

My favorite encourage-mints go to the overworked, often underappreciated, "invisible" store employees. After doing medical transcription for many years, I know the feeling of being chained to my computer, almost becoming a mechanical inhuman part of it. Certainly a grocery store checker must share those feelings at times as they endlessly move items across a beeping scanner.

Into that world I come as a customer. Not a customer focused on myself, but as an undercover detective, searching for someone who needs an encourage-mint. I am not in any checkout line by accident.

Have you ever cringed when watching a rude customer in front of you ~ an emotional bully, spitting out hurtful words like a verbal machine gun, making the clerk feel a little lower than the dust on the floor?

After seeing such a display of anger, think about what words you could say to the employee that would heal the emotional wounds just inflicted. When it is your turn, start with a friendly smile. You can show empathy by telling them it must be difficult to listen to a customer like the one who just left. Look for something they did or said that you can sincerely compliment.

At times, I know you will be surprised by what you say, because that is the Holy Spirit guiding you for that person's needs. Be cautious to keep your conversation simple and sincere. They are being watched by their bosses, electronically or visually, and we do not want them to get in trouble for talking too much. It's easy to get them to smile by including their name from their badge when you say, "thank you." Using their name helps them to feel less like a machine.

Whether your encourage-mint takes 10 minutes of talking, hugging or even a few tears, or is a quick small mint for a checker, the recipient feels better. While we cannot take away all of their pain or suffering in a few minutes, we did what God led us to do and can trust him for the results.

Maybe you are wondering how you can be sure you are really hearing the thoughts of the Holy Spirit. If what he is asking you to do is kind, caring, loving, unselfish and will give the person hope in that moment, then you know it is OK. As you experience more and more of these God encounters, it gets easier to recognize and respond to them.

Have I always succeeded in my quest to give out encourage-mints? No way! At times,   I felt too embarrassed to speak up. At times, I gave in to the demon of hurry and failed to really notice what was happening around me. At times, I wrongly judged someone to not be worthy of my attention.

But when we willingly give out encourage-mints, then our lives become filled with close encounters of the God kind.

Be An Answer To Someone's Prayers

§

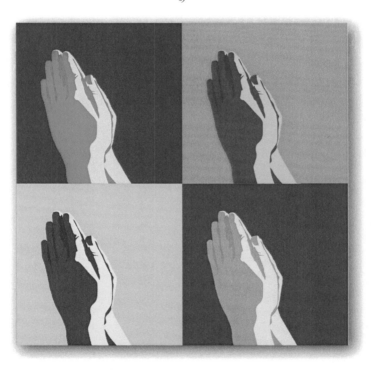

Whether you turn to the right or to the left,

your ears will hear a voice

behind you saying, "This is the way. Walk in it."

Isaiah 30:21 NIV

Few will have the greatness to bend history itself,

but each of us can work

to change a small portion of events.

Robert F. Kennedy

Let no one come to you without leaving happier and better.

Mother Teresa

Years ago I heard a speaker say that we may be the answer to prayers that someone has been waiting for. I must admit my first response was, "doubt it!" Yet this thought kept bugging me. Our brain seems to work like that ~ keeping a thought bouncing around until we finally must do something about it. So my thinking brought up these three questions:

- What if God really could use mixed-up me that way?
- What if God had already used me that way and I just did not realize it?
- What if I started to live by believing I could be an answer to someone's prayer?

These questions started my journey of self-discovery with lots of surprises and "ah-ha, I get it!" moments.

Perhaps my biggest underlying struggle might also be yours. The traumatic events we experience, and the words that wound us so deeply, easily contribute to our feeling inadequate ~ not good enough for God's work. We all know our faults and where we don't measure up to what we think someone else expects of us ~ or what we unfairly expect of ourselves. Who hasn't thought life would be better if we were prettier, taller, smarter, thinner, younger, whatever?

Who am I to think that God could work through me to answer a prayer? Even though the Bible and history tell many stories of unlikely people doing amazing things, I still had doubts about my being worthy. Then I found this life-changing verse:

Who are you to talk back to God? Shall what is formed say to him
who formed it, why did you make me like this?
Does not the potter have the
right to make out of the same lump of clay some
pottery for special purposes
and some for common use? Romans 9:20 NIV

Ouch! Did that ever sound like me. Talking back to God by complaining about how he made me! This revelation definitely brought about repentance ~ changing my mind and going in the opposite direction. I confess to occasionally still thinking negatively about myself, but the Holy Spirit quickly reminds me that I am a child of God with unique DNA from the first joining of cells in my mother's womb. We were carefully designed and created by God ~ not a result of time and chance or evolution.

With that improved mind-set, I moved on to my second question: What if God had already used me to answer a prayer but I didn't see it that way? An amazing part of believing the Holy Spirit lives in me is that I can mentally ask that kind of question and get answers. Maybe not all at once, but coming in bits and pieces as I can absorb them.

To God, there is no dumb question. James 1:5 encourages us that when we need wisdom, insight or GPS (God's Positioning System) directions, just ask, and answers will be revealed to us.

Many of us have often helped others, although not always motivated by believing God is working through us. Yet the idea that what I had done might have been an answer to someone's prayer sent me on a search through the cluttered memory files of my brain to see if it could be true.

Sometimes the answer was obvious. My husband reminded me of a time when he found a wallet on the ground in a city park with nine $100 bills! The address on the driver's license was nearby, so he drove over to the house. The woman who opened the door had red eyes from crying and thanked him several times for returning the money. She asked him to come inside for a moment and showed him an open Bible on her kitchen table. She had been praying for an honest person to return the money, because it was their rent for next month. No doubt she felt his actions were an answer to her prayers.

Another obvious answer happened to me. I read about a new book available with unique ideas to help a person in charge of a Sunday school program at a church. So I ordered it and put it on a shelf, basically forgetting I ordered it. One morning at breakfast, I was convinced the Holy Spirit told me to get that book and take it over to our church (20 minute drive each way) and give it to the lady in charge of the children's classes.

When I arrived without an appointment, she said to come to her office, where she was having a meeting with several of her teachers. I apologized for interrupting and told her I had ordered the book and felt I should bring it over right then. They all looked shocked and some smiled, so she let me in on their surprise. Just a few minutes earlier, my friend had told them about that exact book and how much she wanted to order it, as it seemed to offer good ideas. So when I walked in with that exact book, she said it was a great example of someone listening to the promptings of the Holy Spirit and following through with action.

Had she actually "prayed" for that book? Probably not in the formal way we think of as prayer. But she did want the book, and evidently God wanted her to have it in the way I provided.

Which makes me wonder ~ do we really _need_ to know if someone actually prayed for what we did for them? A quick dictionary check reveals that prayer can also mean hope, wish, anticipate, look forward to or yearn for. When you add those, the evidence for our being an answer to prayer grows and grows. Seek and you will find surprising examples from your past.

Which leads to my third question: What if I started to live by believing I could be an answer to prayer? Then I would be like George in *It's A Wonderful Life*, a classic Christmas movie.

In the first half of the movie, we see George getting depressed as other people earn more money, get to travel when he stays home to run the family business, become a national war hero, and worst of all, see the dishonest nasty guy be in a position of power. George feels so worthless that he thinks everyone would have been better off if he had never lived.

So God sends him an angel to show him what life for others would have been like if he had not lived. The answers are shocking, to George, and to us. Many families would not have been able to afford the homes he built. His brother would not have been a hero and saved everyone on a ship because George had not saved his life as a kid. After seeing more examples, George finally understands how God has been using him. Now he wants to live.

Not only did George learn he had a wonderful life, but we are reminded that our lives matter greatly to God, because He works through us to answer the prayers of more people than we could imagine!

A unique aspect of my life involves being a resource person ~ often sharing the specific information someone needs to solve their problem exactly at the right time ~ another way to be an answer to their prayers. How is that possible? I am intentional in being an information pack rat ~ a hoarder of tidbits, factoids, scraps, crumbs, fragments and other assorted pieces. I hesitate to admit I occasionally print the "About Us" page on a website and file it in one of my many resource notebooks (ordinary three ring-binders). My office is littered with those notebooks, crammed onto bookshelves and all other available spaces.

Has it been worthwhile? Absolutely! I read about a diabetic pain clinic in a major city about 150 miles from us that used new methods. When a friend told me she suffered from that kind of pain, I told her about the clinic. Yet as often will happen when you are an answer to someone's prayers, that someone may never let you know you helped. But when I happened to see her at a Christmas party a year later, she gave me a hug and apologized for not telling me sooner that going to that clinic had greatly reduced her pain!

We resource junkies live for those moments!!

Once I read an amazing inspiring book about dealing with chronic pain and a "new normal," the kind of life a person might have after a serious accident or illness. I had told several people about the book but never heard if they read it. Then last summer when a young lady was visiting us, we talked about all the ways her life had changed since she had been in a serious car accident, resulting in lifelong disabilities.

After telling her about the book, she said it would be OK for me to order it online and have it sent to her apartment. I knew it would be an answer to her prayers for how to cope better, but I did not expect any feedback.

To my wonderful surprise and joy, *while writing this chapter*, I received a heartfelt thank you note from her, saying:

"It's amazing the confirmation from that book of what God has shown and taught me these past six years living through the accident aftermath. I love the 'new normal' idea.   I shared the book with my Dad and was surprised when he took it home with him to read. Thanks again for sending me the book."

No doubt I have collected more information than I will ever give away, but getting a thank you note like above makes it all worthwhile. Consider saving such notes for the days when you will wonder if what you do for others is worth your time and effort.

Whether you give a prayer bear, an encourage-mint to a store checker, or trust the Holy Spirit as you become the answer to someone's prayers, networking with God adds purpose and significance to our lives and impacts others beyond our imagination.

A story about being an answer to someone's prayers

§

from the second season of the West Wing TV series episode 10 ~ first aired December 20, 2000

§

(After Josh faces the reality of the emotional scars he will always have from being shot, his friend and boss, Leo, told him this story, to demonstrate what true friendship means.)

A guy is walking down a street when he falls into a deep hole. The sides are so steep, he can't get out by himself.

A doctor passes by and the guy yells out, "Hey, you! Can you help me out?"

The doctor writes a prescription and throws it into the hole and walks on by.

Then a priest comes along and the guy calls out, "Father, I fell in this hole. Can you help me out?"

The priest writes a prayer on a piece of paper, throws it into the hole and keeps on walking by the hole.

Then a friend walks by and the guy calls out again, "Hey, my friend, can you help me out?"

and the friend jumps in the hole with him.

So the guy says, "Are you stupid? Now we're both down here!" and his friend says,

"Yeah, but I've been down here before and I know the way out."

Enjoying 4Th Quarter Living

I am a little pencil in the hand of a writing God,

who is sending his love letter to the world.

Mother Teresa

You are never too old to set another goal or to dream a new dream.

C.S. Lewis

Not only was the teacher wise, but he also imparted knowledge

to the people. He pondered and searched out and set in order

many proverbs. The teacher searched to find just the right words,

and what he wrote was upright and true.

Ecclesiastes 12:9 NIV

HAVE YOU EVER WATCHED A fourth-quarter comeback in football? The game score reflects what seems like a lopsided, sure win at the end of the third quarter. Then the underdog team suddenly comes to life!

They make an interception that turns into a touchdown. They sack the quarterback several times. A perfectly thrown and caught pass for 56 yards results in another exciting touchdown. The crowd comes to life, stops booing and starts cheering.

Makes you wonder where *this* team was during the first three quarters! It all ends with an onside kick that favors the underdog, and they win! Lots of celebrating. **

That's how I feel about this time in my life.

Let's consider that our lives are divided into four quarters:

1 to 20   first quarter

21 to 40   second quarter

41 to 60   third quarter

61 to 80   fourth quarter

80+   overtime

That would put me in my fourth quarter.

When we were teens and twenty-somethings, we could not imagine ourselves as "seniors" ~ but if we live long enough, we do grow older. Like that underdog team, I choose to do what I can to make this time exciting.

Maybe, like me, you have reached your fourth quarter with re-grets, missed chances to be what you had hoped, plans that failed, sickness, loss or unfair rejection that could make you feel like that underdog team, just enduring 15 more minutes of football before the sure defeat of boring old age.

But any of us can still become winners, making our fourth quarter our best quarter. Finishing well can and does happen. History records many people who began their most creative and significant accomplishments in the later years of their lives.

Don't be like all of us have been at least once ~ turning off the game on TV because you were sure your team was losing, only to hear the next day that you missed their amazing comeback.

Because you kept reading this book to the finish, you get to learn about the trick play that gave the underdog team their go-ahead touchdown ~ they were willing to try something new ~ something unexpected ~ because they didn't give up hope.

Perhaps you are facing what seems like an insurmountable end-of-game situation. You are down to only 4 seconds on the clock and could easily give up – but don't do it!! You might face opposition, like the entire marching band coming onto the field to distract you before the game is over. Just keep running toward the end zone to score a touchdown.**

God never gives up on us! No matter how many times we fail, I'm sure he enjoys throwing us a game-winning pass in our 4th quarter, sending us into overtime years.

** If you enjoy football, these true stories of two dramatic come-from-behind wins demonstrate the importance of not giving up in the 4th quarter.

§

Let's consider the game between the University of California Golden Bears and the Stanford Cardinals on Saturday, November 20, 1982. John Elway led the Bears in his last college game. He threw a 29-yard completion that got the team close enough to kick a field goal with only 8 seconds left. They could have run the clock down more but the coach wanted extra time to kick a second field goal if the first one missed, which it did not. With only 4 seconds left, Stanford was now ahead 20-19. The team celebrated a bit too much and received a 15-yard penalty on the kickoff. As one announcer said, "Only a miracle can save the Bears now."

The Bears caught the pass and ran with it for a few yards and then the runner was tackled, but not before he had lateraled the ball (not a forward pass but legal), and the team proceeded to do this four more times. As this was happening, the Stanford marching band took to the field to celebrate, as did some of the Stanford players, both of which were against the rules because the game was not over.

The last runner for the Bears had to zig-zag through the band and their instruments until reaching the end zone, where the referee signaled a touchdown! The Bears had won the game! This remains perhaps the most exciting and unexpected ending of any game in college football history. It proved that the Bears players would not give up and kept going and going, eventually stunning everyone.

https://www.youtube.com/watch?v=0wR3r7yJqbE

https://en.wikipedia.org/wiki/The_Play

§

A more recent example of a miraculous 4th quarter comeback happened on Sunday, January 18, 2015, between the Seattle Seahawks and the Green Bay Packers. The Seahawks' first three quarters were dismal and disappointing. They had a 16-point deficit going into the fourth quarter.

"Outplayed much of the game and plagued by five turnovers, (four of them passes to Kearse that were intercepted) the Seahawks trailed 16-7 with 2:09 minutes remaining in the 4th quarter. That's when the quarterback Wilson ran for a 1-yard touchdown. They recovered a bobbled onside kick at the 50 and Lynch ran for a 24-yard touchdown. The 2-point conversion pass was caught, making the score 22-19. Amazingly, they had scored 15 points in 44 seconds! Then the Packers came back for a field goal with14 seconds to go, sending the game into overtime." (from www.nfl.com)

In the overtime, Wilson completed three passes, the third to the one man who had such a bad game, Jermaine Kearse. Wilson did not give up on his best receiver, throwing him the game-winning overtime touchdown pass.

Our Response

§

the world beats on us

cruel words kill our spirits

people always finding fault

until no one meets their standard

how do we of faith survive?

do we hide from people who hurt us?

do we fight the evil and injustice?

do we allow our fears to limit us?

Jesus' words reminds us

do not be afraid

be at peace

for I have overcome the world

our response becomes clear

reflect Jesus' light and love

into their dark and fear-filled lives

pray for our enemies

that some day

they may know Jesus

he lived, suffered and died

as the son of God and a perfect man

so on the cross he could tell us

father forgive them

for they know not what they do

remember, Jesus promised us

I go to prepare a place for you

an eternal home

with no sickness, sadness

tears or death

so do not be discouraged

by the evil in our world

Jesus will never leave us

not in this life

not in eternity to come

Encourage-Mints is available as a Kindle ebook:

http://www.amazon.com/dp/B009L8LSCG#

Contact the author: carol@basicfamily.org

Submit your e-mint story or tell me about the book you publish:

emints@basicfamily.org

§

FREE ONLINE ENCOURAGE-MINTS FOR YOU:

God Loves You. This is His love letter to you.

http://www.fathersloveletter.com/   (7-minute video)

§

What it means to accept Jesus and follow him:

www.billygraham.org

New Life Birth Certificate:

www.newbeliever.info/images/nlbc.pdf

Your new life in Christ is real and will last for eternity....

faith is a choice....don't depend on your feelings....

be encouraged by these verses of promise to you

    http://www.basicfamily.org/promise-verses.pdf

31 days of Encourage-Mints (one verse for each day)

    www.basicfamily.org/everses.pdf

31 days of Encourage-Mints (one quotation for each day)

    www.basicfamily.org/equotes.pdf

Carol's favorite quotations:

    www.basicfamily.org/favorites.pdf

Encourage-Mint lists from this web site (2011-2014)

    http://www.basicfamily.org/encourage-mints.htm

Bible verses about living with one another:

    www.basicfamily.org/one-anothers.pdf

Bible verses that we are children of God:

    www.basicfamily.org/child-of-God-verses.pdf

Time of Prayer – pray for your city on the 1st day of each month:

    www.basicfamily.org/TOP.pdf